# WHAT GOD DOES WHEN MEN PRAY

## A SMALL GROUP DISCUSSION GUIDE

## WILLIAM CARR PEEL

**NAVPRESS**
BRINGING TRUTH TO LIFE
NavPress Publishing Group
P.O. Box 35001, Colorado Springs, Colorado 80935

The Navigators is an international Christian organization.
Our mission is to reach, disciple, and equip people to know
Christ and to make Him known through successive genera-
tions. We envision multitudes of diverse people in the
United States and every other nation who have a passionate
love for Christ, live a lifestyle of sharing Christ's love, and
multiply spiritual laborers among those without Christ.

NavPress is the publishing ministry of The Navigators.
NavPress publications help believers learn biblical truth and
apply what they learn to their lives and ministries. Our mission is to stimulate spiritual formation among our readers.

© 1993 by William Carr Peel
ISBN 08910-97295

Printed in the United States of America

8 9 10 11 12 13 14 15 16 17 18 / 99 98 97 96

# CONTENTS

*To James Carr Peel,*
*my earthly father and inspiration in prayer,*
*who prayed daily for me and forty-nine others*
*before he went to be with our heavenly Father*

# FOREWORD

The need for men of prayer, integrity, conviction, and action is greater than ever. Our churches and families need men who are committed to prayer. Our communities need Christians who will stand up and proclaim Jesus Christ with conviction and compassion. A world with misplaced values needs men who are fueled by God's Spirit and who are compelled to bring light into a dark world.

Promise Keepers began in 1990 because of these needs, for the purpose of motivating Christian men to make and keep their promises to Jesus Christ, their families, their churches, their communities, and their friends.

What is a "promise keeper"? Promise keepers are:

▶ Men of prayer and students of God's Word

▶ Men of sincerity and honesty

▶ Men who are accountable to one another

▶ Men who express honor and care for their wives

▶ Men who father and nurture their children

▶ Men who actively support their pastor and church

▶ Men who champion the cause of the needy and fatherless

It's not by accident that being "men of prayer" tops this list. We want to proclaim loud and clear that "A MAN'S MAN IS A GODLY MAN." A godly man is a man who is dependent on God and who expresses his dependence in a life of prayer. Only men of prayer will be able to access the necessary power to effect change in themselves and maximize their abilities to impact others.

Most people try to cope with little or no spiritual food. Their lives are often characterized by ups and downs, highs and lows, mountains and valleys. They really can't deal with the adversity or even good fortune that comes into their lives.

A relationship with God, strengthened by prayer and Scripture, is the answer to this dilemma. I am awed by the reality that I can freely converse with Almighty God—the Creator of the universe—through His Son, Jesus Christ! At any place, during any time, I can freely pray to Him as a son talks to his father.

Through daily prayer and reading the Bible, Almighty God softens a man's heart, shapes his character, roots out sin in his life, and gives him direction and purpose. A life of prayer is foundational for a man who wants to run on all cylinders for God.

I have a vivid picture in my mind of entire stadiums of men, gathered together at the same time throughout the country, proclaiming Jesus Christ as Lord and praying together as one man. God is looking for men who are "red hot" for Jesus. His eyes are moving "to and fro" looking for men who have a full passion for the gospel message.

May we fervently grapple before God because of the present condition of the moral fabric of the men in this nation. The Lord is calling Christian men to lead a new uprising of men filled with God's Spirit. This uprising will begin only if men will go to their knees with other men and seek the Lord with true intensity. I pray that *What God Does When Men Pray* will encourage you in this way.

—BILL MCCARTNEY

# ACKNOWLEDGMENTS

This study was written for the 200-plus men who have been involved in small groups in Tyler, Texas. They are not only my target, they are also my inspiration and encouragement. Two groups deserve special thanks for putting up with me every week, for years:

The Tuesday morning group—Frank Budde, Don Guinn, Richard Harvey, Bill Hughes, James Milstead, Tom Ramey, Shirley Simons, Watson Simons, Harold Smotherman, and Dan Woldert.

The Thursday noon group—Jerry Atherton, Robert Bratton, John Breedlove, Doug Cordell, Brad Harvey, and Al Jasper.

Special thanks to five men who are my true partners in the business of prayer: John Breedlove, Steve Keuer, Tom Ramey, Watson Simons, and Harold Smotherman.

Special thanks also to Bill Garrison who taught me where the action is: with men in the marketplace; to my wonderful wife, Kathy, who taught me to pray for simple things; and to my three young men—John, Joel, and James—who make my life a joy.

# ABOUT PROMISE KEEPERS

Promise Keepers is an organization dedicated to motivating men toward greater strength and Christlike masculinity.

Promise Keepers sponsors men's conferences in regional locations and various churches around the country. The annual Promise Keepers National Men's Conference is held each July in Boulder, Colorado.

Promise Keepers seeks to be a supply line to the local church, helping to encourage and assist pastors and ministry leaders in calling men to an accountable relationship with Jesus Christ and with one another. Promise Keepers wants to provide men's materials (like this book) as well as seminars and the annual conference to emphasize the godly conviction, integrity, and action each of us needs.

Please join us in helping one another be the kind of men God wants us to be. Write or call our offices today.

Promise Keepers
P.O. Box 18376
Boulder, CO 80308

1-800-228-3100
or
1-303-421-2800

# BEFORE YOU BEGIN

If you want to see a group of highly successful, hard-nosed businessmen squirm, just mention two words: "Let's pray." Most men I know rank public prayer somewhere between getting a root canal and receiving a registered letter from the IRS. Over the past twenty years, I've met with countless men in small groups. We found discussing the Bible in open transparency easy compared to leaping the prayer barrier. Even when another group member would lead our study, I would usually get the nod: "Bill, close our time in prayer."

Several years ago my dad gave me a worn copy of E.M. Bounds' 1911 classic *The Preacher and Prayer* (now *Power Through Prayer*). Reading it not only changed my prayer life, but made me realize I was inflicting damage by always being responsible for the praying in the groups. Bounds' words hit me hard:

> We are constantly on a stretch if not a strain, to devise new methods, new plans, new organizations to advance the Church and secure enlargement and efficiency for the gospel. . . . Men are God's method. The Church is looking for better methods; God is looking for better men. . . . The Holy Ghost does not flow through methods, but through men. He does not come on machinery, but men. He does not anoint plans, but men—men of prayer.

Somewhere along the way, most men opted out of the prayer loop—leaving the job to women and preachers. Perhaps that's one of the reasons why 53,000 people exit the doors of churches in the United States and Europe every Sunday and never return. It's not only our churches that suffer because men do not pray, but our homes and businesses as well. It's time men learn to pray—and learn to pray together.

In Matthew 18:19-20, Christ makes an astounding promise we cannot afford to leave on the table:

> "I tell you that if two of you on earth agree about anything you ask for, it will be done for you by my Father in

heaven. For where two or three come together in my name, there am I with them."

## ABOUT THIS STUDY

What began as three pages of notes on group prayer evolved into the book you now have in your hands. This is certainly not meant to be an exhaustive treatment—as if anyone could exhaust the subject of prayer—but as a begining experiment for men. Think of the subtitle of this study as more like "Talking to Daddy," rather than "How to Obviate a Vacuous Verbal Intercourse with the Omnipotent Deity."

Although any person, a married couple, or a mixed-gender group could benefit from this study, it was written to entice and initiate groups of men, step by step, into the great adventure of praying together. It's designed to help men "taste and see that the Lord is good," and then drink as deeply as they dare.

This study is divided into eight sessions, which are designed to be covered in eight weeks or whatever pace the group finds most beneficial. Between group meetings, participants can divide their study time over five days. Daily breakdowns are indicated in each session. Most of the daily sections can be completed in fifteen to twenty minutes. When the group meets, each participant can discuss his insights from the "Time for Thought" section.

## LEADING THE GROUP

If you have picked up this book, chances are that God has a great adventure in store for you and a group of your associates. I urge you to follow God's prompting and take the challenge. You may have chosen this study for a small group you already meet with regularly, or perhaps you'll want to start from scratch and invite a group of men to join you in the adventure. In my experience, groups of six to twelve men work best. If you have more than twelve, consider dividing into smaller groups for discussion.

If you are starting a new group, don't think you must invite only mature Christians. Even sincere seekers will find the topic fascinating. The only necessary requirements are:

▶ A commitment to be present for eight weeks

▶ A willingness to do the assignments

▶ A desire to discover God in prayer

▶ A promise to allow each group member to develop at his own pace

As you plan the meetings, take time to survey the material and prepare to lead the discussion. Although group members can take turns leading the discussion, one person should be in charge of the logistics.

One very important aspect of this study is the "Thirty-Day Prayer Experiment." Since this is done with a partner, the group organizer should think ahead about how best to break the group into pairs. He will need to follow the instructions carefully on pages 89-90. Although leadership may be rotated, the organizer should lead the report-back sections and prayer times and point out assignments for the next week.

Let me offer one warning: *Be alert for obstacles that keep you from actually praying.* I have found it all too easy to let time escape—allowing only quick, tack-on-the-end prayer. Always keep the central purpose of the group in mind, and make sure to budget plenty of time for prayer.

## LET ME KNOW WHAT HAPPENS
I hope you'll give me the privilege of hearing how God meets you in this adventure. Please let me know about your answered prayers and anything you discover that helps men pray together. Write to me:

Bill Peel
Foundations for Living
P.O. Box 5100
Tyler, TX 75712

# THE UNCOMFORTABLE BUSINESS OF PRAYER

In the fall of 1984, I traveled with my good friend Bill Byrd, president of Sweet Shop Candies in Fort Worth, Texas, to the interior of Mexico to meet J. K. Adams. We observed firsthand his work at Emmaus Christian Academy in Hermosillo, a bustling town of a half-million people and the capital of the state of Sonora. Though I had studied Spanish in school and had even worked side by side with Mexican nationals on a construction project, my Spanish was not just rusty, it had virtually oxidized. I remembered how to ask a person's name and age, the time, and the location of the rest room, but I was shocked at my inability to communicate with the people. However, as long as J. K. was there all was well.

The second day of our visit, we went on a short tour of the city and ended up at the downtown square near the capitol and university. Wanting to see the sights up close, Bill and I talked J. K. into leaving us there to explore for forty-five minutes while he ran an errand to the post office. Feeling rather brave, we did a quick number on the capitol, market, and cathedral. At the end of forty-five minutes we were dutifully back at our rendezvous, waiting for our host. Thirty minutes passed, and I began to get a little

*Please read thoughtfully, and then answer the questions that follow in the "Time for Thought" section before your first group meeting.*

uneasy. Since Hermosillo is off the beaten path for *touristas*, few of the people who walked past us spoke more English than I did Spanish. Polite shrugs greeted our attempts to get directions to the post office.

The minutes dripped by like molasses as we waited and wondered what to do. An hour passed, and I grew increasingly uncomfortable realizing that only one person knew where we were (and we weren't sure what had happened to him). I will never forget the sense of isolation I felt, trapped behind a language and culture barrier. What a relief finally to see our friend who had been unavoidably detained with no way to let us know.

The feeling I've described is not unlike what many people feel when praying in front of others—the culture is foreign, the language is strange. They can't wait to escape the situation and get back to their own familiar world where people talk to someone they can see, in a dialect they can understand.

There is no doubt about it. Prayer takes some getting used to for most of us. Plenty of artificial barriers, which have nothing to do with the essence of prayer, make us feel like outsiders. Religious traditions—such as the use of a special language, being in a certain posture, the necessity to recite certain formulas, or being in a specific place—all needlessly keep us from experiencing the joy of prayer.

> *Prayer is like a foreign land. When we go there, we go as tourists. Like most tourists, we feel uncomfortable and out of place. Like most tourists, we therefore move on before too long and go somewhere else.*
> —Robert MacAfee Brown

On the other hand, there are genuine obstacles blocking all of us. Prayer involves communicating with another world, a spiritual realm that is as real as the physical realm, yet we cannot see or touch it. Prayer also involves talking to Someone who is very different from us. Not only is He vastly superior, He is absolutely holy while at the same time openly gracious.

Those who are able to break through the barriers to prayer, both real and contrived, find a world that is as substantial as the one in which they eat, sleep, and work—a world where they realize they belong, talking to Someone they have always longed to know with a desire that is too deep for words.

This study is about discovering the adventure not only of prayer, but of praying together with other men. In a sense, it is like a new citizens' class. Everyone is a learner and fumbles a bit with the words. No one knows it all.

Together, you will learn some of the great privileges, responsibilities, and ways to access the resources that belong to every citizen of Heaven. You will learn about God Himself and what He wants to do with praying men. My hope is that you will stop feeling like a tourist, settle down, and enjoy the presence of God. Prayer can become as natural and meaningful as joining a conversation with your friends—even *more* meaningful, for God Himself joins your circle and graciously calls you "friend."

## TIME FOR THOUGHT

1. Think back through what you have just read. Have you ever experienced the feeling about prayer that Robert MacAfee Brown described on page 16?
   - ☐ Never
   - ☐ Always
   - ☐ When I am alone
   - ☐ When I am with others
   - ☐ When I am with certain people
   - ☐ Other (name it): _____
   _____
   _____

2. If prayer has ever caused you to feel like a "tourist," why do you think you were uncomfortable?

Use the options suggested with the following questions to get your thinking started. Don't let them limit your responses. Be sure to write down any "other" answers.

**GROUP LEADER:** Discuss these questions in the group after you have read the beginning text aloud together.

☐ I felt like an outsider.
☐ I didn't know the lingo.
☐ I didn't know what to say.
☐ Other (name it): _____

_____

_____

3. Read Matthew 18:19-20. What is your first impression of this promise? (We will study the passage in detail in session 4.) _____

_____

_____

_____

_____

_____

4. What do you personally hope to gain from this study?_____

_____

_____

_____

_____

_____

## GETTING THE MOST OUT OF THIS STUDY

*What God Does When Men Pray* is designed to be completed in eight weeks, though it can be compacted or expanded according to the group's needs and desires. Each session has a content section followed by discussion questions. In each session, you will also find boxed instructions for group members. These will help you break the study into six daily portions, which you will be able to complete in ten to twenty minutes.

### Four Guidelines

As a participant you should be willing to agree to these actions:

▶ Commit yourself to completing the assignments before the group meeting.

- Make the group meeting a nonnegotiable item in your schedule.

- Be an active participant in group discussion and prayer to the extent you personally feel comfortable.

- Pray personally for the members of the group.

## The Benefits

If you want to experience more of the privilege and power of prayer, this study is for you. You will:

- Understand the simplicity of prayer.

- Discover what God can do through praying men.

- Identify the barriers to effective prayer in your life.

- Understand the importance of prayer to your work.

- See God's eagerness to answer our prayers.

- Discover the awesome power of group prayer.

- Develop a network of men who will pray with and for each other.

## THE THIRTY-DAY PRAYER EXPERIMENT

The "Thirty-Day Prayer Experiment" is an opportunity to discover the power of prayer. See the instructions on pages 89-90 and read through the steps.

The "Experiment" involves a partner. My partner for the next thirty days will be:

Name:

Address:

Phone:

**GROUP LEADER:**
Discuss which of the six benefits attracts each person most.

**GROUP LEADER:**
Explain the concept of a prayer chain. Fill out the "Prayer Chain" form together (see appendix, page 94), making sure everyone uses the same order. If a group member is absent, make sure he copies the information on his "Prayer Chain" form at the next group meeting.
Spend the balance of your group time setting up the "Thirty-Day Prayer Experiment." Read through the text on page 89 aloud together. Ask each group member to select a prayer partner in the group and call him with requests in two days.
At the end of the group time, you should close with a short prayer.

## ASSIGNMENT FOR NEXT WEEK

Read the text for session 2 and work through all of the questions. Be prepared to discuss your thoughts together with the group.

Meet with your prayer partner before the next meeting, if possible, to exchange prayer requests.

In case of the need for emergency prayer, use the prayer chain.

# BECOMING PRAYING MEN

*Financial prosperity and spiritual poverty*—
most of the time they have existed together in the
history of our country. I found it instructive to
watch the rise of the spiritual temperature in
Texas as oil prices fell during the late 1980s. On
the whole, the United States shows little sign of
spiritual up-turn apart from tough times.

Day One: Read
thoughtfully, and
jot down any
questions or
comments the
text brings to
your mind.

In a yearly study sponsored by the American
Council on Education and conducted by UCLA's
Education Research Institute, 75 percent of the
college freshmen in 1987 considered "being well
off financially" as an "essential" or "major life
goal." When financial success becomes the con-
trolling goal of life, it usually skews a person's
whole value system, bringing devastating results.

Michael Korda writes in *Success*,

It's O.K. to be greedy.

It's O.K. to be ambitious.

It's O.K. to look out for Number One.

It's O.K. to have a good time.

It's O.K. to be Machiavellian (if you can
get away with it).

It's O.K. to recognize that honesty is not
always the best policy (provided you don't
go around saying so).

It's O.K. to be a winner.
And, it's always O.K. to be rich.[1]

The conflict with Christian values is obvious. Although the Bible never has a problem with wealth, it warns against the stranglehold misplaced priorities can have on our lives.

Things now are not so different from the mid-1800s. Men were chasing the buck and often catching it. They were keeping God at a safe but convenient distance—in the church building. Just as now, things were not altogether positive economically. In August 1857, the Ohio Life Insurance and Trust Company failed due to speculation and investment in rails and mining. The resulting panic, which affected the banks in large cities, had a sobering effect on the business community. Every businessman was anxious about what this meant economically. Some men, however, were conscious of what it meant spiritually.

> *We have been the recipients of the choicest bounties of Heaven; we have been preserved these many years in peace and prosperity; we have grown in numbers, wealth, and power as no other nation has ever grown. But we have forgotten God. We have forgotten the gracious hand which preserved us in peace and multiplied and enriched us, and we have vainly imagined, in the deceitfulness of our hearts, that all these blessings were produced by some superior wisdom and virtue of our own. Intoxicated with unbroken success, we have become too self-sufficient to feel the necessity of redeeming and preserving grace, too proud to pray to the God that made us.*
> —Abraham Lincoln, 1863, "Proclamation of a Day of National Humiliation, Fasting, and Prayer"

## WHAT HAPPENS WHEN MEN PRAY?
While many men felt concern about the state of their neighbor's soul in the 1850s, one layman did something significant—*he prayed!* As a result, more men prayed. And, beginning to be visible in 1857, the wind of the Spirit of God swept through our country, radically changing

men's lives for four decades.

We do not usually know who prayed, who was the human cause behind the divine effect, but in 1857 we do. A church janitor named Jeremiah Lamphier advertised a prayer meeting scheduled to meet in the Dutch Reformed Church in Manhattan. Six people showed up the first week, fourteen the next, and twenty-three the next. They decided to meet every day. Soon filling their first location, they spilled over to the Methodist church, and then to every public building in downtown New York. Horace Greeley's reporter could get around to only twelve meetings during the noon hour, but counted *6,100 men—praying men!*

A landslide of revival began that did not wane until the nineteenth century neared an end. As a result, millions came to know Christ. They knew Him not as a religious figure merely to honor once a week, but as a Master worthy to be followed every day of life. He was a personal Savior who cared enough to give His life to deliver men from the worst poverty of all, *spiritual poverty*. Eternity is different for many of our great-grandparents because men prayed.

*Denver Post*—January 20, 1905
"Entire city pauses for prayer even at the high tide of business."
The marts of trade were deserted between noon and two o'clock this afternoon, and all worldly affairs were forgotten, and the entire city was given over to meditation of higher things. The Spirit of the Almighty pervaded every nook. Going to and coming from the great meetings, thousands of men and women radiated this Spirit which filled them, and the clear Colorado sunshine was made brighter by the reflected glow of the light of God shining from happy faces. Seldom has such a remarkable sight been witnessed—an entire great city, in the middle of a busy weekday, bowing before the throne of heaven and asking and receiving the blessing of the King of the Universe.

Revival occurred again in our grandparents' day soon after the turn of the century, again because men prayed. Entire business districts closed up shop at lunchtime for prayer. Thousands transferred their confidence in themselves to Christ to gain eternal life.

## CAN IT HAPPEN TODAY?

Even though our present economic climate is hauntingly similar, it is hard to imagine something like this happening today in the success-obsessed culture we live in. Can men put Christ above commerce? Can we see tens, even hundreds of our own friends, neighbors, and business associates come to Christ? Of course the answer is "yes." We have the same God who delights to forgive sin and transform lives. The question is, "Will men pray?" No, the real question is, *"Will I pray?"* Will you?

Think for a moment of the man who goes to work, whether in the work place or the worship place, seeing himself as a tool in the hand of God, asking for wisdom, guidance, and effectiveness in doing his daily work. Such a man brings the resources of Jesus Christ to bear on whatever task at which he works. Prayer and work flow together as naturally as conversation between fellow workers. Prayer makes the resources of Heaven available to us for any earthly task. In fact, apart from the participation of Christ's life in and through us, we will never reach the potential for which God designed us.

A cobbler named William Carey, overwhelmed by the spiritual darkness in foreign lands, became the founder of modern missions. A parliamentarian, William Wilberforce brought about the end of slavery in the British Empire. Church custodian Jeremiah Lamphier initiated revival in 1857. With a group of fellow Christians, Valdemar Hvidt, a Danish attorney, all but eliminated unemployment in 1930s Denmark during the Great Depression.

I wonder what God would do today about hunger, homelessness, drug addiction, and decaying family life. What if a group of men determined to pray and seek God's help and guidance to tackle these problems that burden the hearts of God and men?

> *Adversity is sometimes hard on a man; but for one man that can stand prosperity, there are a hundred that will stand adversity.*
> —Thomas Carlisle

## TIME FOR THOUGHT

1. Read Hosea 13:6. Why do you think that financial prosperity and spiritual poverty so often go together?
   - ☐ Pride
   - ☐ Distraction
   - ☐ Ingratitude
   - ☐ No sense of need
   - ☐ Cares of the world
   - ☐ Distorted perspective
   - ☐ Wealth and spirituality can't exist together.
   - ☐ Other (name it): _____
   _____
   _____

2. What do you think happens to us spiritually when we succeed or become prosperous?
   - ☐ We think that we are responsible.
   - ☐ We don't feel a daily need for God.
   - ☐ We are distracted with the responsibilities of preserving our success.
   - ☐ Other: _____
   _____
   _____

3. Can you think of people you have known who seemed to lose their spiritual edge when they achieved success? What, if anything, did you learn from them? _____
   _____
   _____
   _____
   _____

Day Two: Respond to the following questions, and be prepared to discuss your answers. Use the suggested answers only to help you get started with your responses.

**GROUP LEADER:** Read the Scripture passages aloud in the group and discuss the questions.

4. Do you personally know of any exceptions to Carlisle's rule (page 25)? Explain. _____

_____

_____

_____

_____

5. Read Psalm 23. Who is really responsible for our success or prosperity? Who does David give credit to in this psalm? _____

_____

6. How has success or failure affected your spiritual life? How has it affected your prayers? Choose one of the statements below and explain your answer.
   ☐ Success has not affected my spiritual life.
   ☐ Success has affected my life.
   ☐ Failure has affected my life.
   ☐ Failure has not affected my spiritual life.

   _____

   _____

   _____

   _____

7. When are you most likely to pray?
   ☐ After disasters
   ☐ During hard times
   ☐ When things go well
   ☐ As daily problems arise
   ☐ Other: _____

   _____

8. What do you think it would take for prayer to become a vital priority in your life?
   ☐ Hard times
   ☐ Discipline
   ☐ More faith
   ☐ Personal failure
   ☐ Realizing my need for God
   ☐ Other: _____

   _____

9. What thought drives you as you go to work?
   ☐ Survival
   ☐ Significance
   ☐ Getting ahead
   ☐ Self-fulfillment
   ☐ Earning a living
   ☐ Getting to the top
   ☐ Providing a service to my fellowman
   ☐ Worshiping God and serving my
      fellowman
   ☐ Other: _____

10. Read Colossians 3:22–4:6. Have you ever
    thought of yourself as a tool in God's hands
    as you do your daily work? Explain. _____
    _____
    _____
    _____
    _____
    _____

11. Have you ever thought of yourself as working
    for God in your daily work?
    ☐ Furthest thing from my mind!
    ☐ I didn't know He was interested.
    ☐ That is why I go to work every day.
    ☐ That would really affect the way I do my
       work.
    ☐ Other: _____

12. How important do you think the quality of
    your work is to God?
    ☐ Crucial
    ☐ Fairly important
    ☐ Somewhat important
    ☐ Not significant
    ☐ Not important if I have a quality spiritual
       life
    ☐ Other: _____

13. What would you say is the first thing God wants of employees and employers who are serious about Him?
☐ Respect others
☐ Do quality work
☐ Quit work and go to seminary
☐ Do your work as an act of worship
☐ See work as primarily an evangelistic platform
☐ Give less time to work so you can spend more time on "spiritual things"
☐ Other: _____

_____

14. What does knowing God's priority do to your concept of your daily work?
☐ Gives my work real dignity
☐ Helps me realize how important my work is to God
☐ Shows how important daily work is to my ministry
☐ Other: _____

_____

**Day Five**

15. Read Titus 2:9-10. How important to God is your ethical behavior in the work place?
☐ Crucial
☐ Fairly important
☐ Somewhat important
☐ Not significant
☐ Not important as long as I "pay my dues" at church
☐ Other: _____

_____

16. What is the biggest ethical issue you face every day in your work?_____

_____
_____
_____
_____
_____

17. Can you envision yourself watching for the opportunity to influence those who work around you daily?
    ☐ This is hard to imagine.
    ☐ I don't understand how this works.
    ☐ This would really affect the way I do my work.
    ☐ Other: _____

    _____

18. Read Colossians 4:2-6 again. In your daily work, what would knowing that you are God's tool mean in your . . .
    direction and goals? _____

    _____
    _____
    _____
    _____

    relationships with coworkers?_____

    _____
    _____
    _____

    successes? _____

    _____
    _____
    _____

    failures?_____

    _____
    _____
    _____
    _____

Day Six

19. How would the idea of being God's tool affect your prayers?
    ☐ No effect
    ☐ I see how much I need God's help and will be more serious about prayer.
    ☐ I can pray about things that I did not know God was concerned about before.

☐ I need to pray about everything I do at work.

☐ Other: _____

_____

**GROUP LEADER:**
Ask how the "Prayer Experiment" is going. Go over the assignment, then ask for a volunteer to close in prayer.

## ASSIGNMENT FOR NEXT WEEK

Read the text for session 3 and work through all of the questions. Be prepared to discuss your thoughts with the group.

Touch base by phone with your prayer partner.

Begin adding items to the "Personal Worry List" on page 95 as they come to mind.

---

NOTE
1. Michael Korda, *Success* (New York: Random House, 1977), pages 4-5.

# WHAT IS PRAYER?

In Washington, D.C., the name of the game is direct access to power. The *gold ring* of success is an open door to the President. Salary and title mean nothing in comparison with an entree to the Oval Office.

Day One: Read thoughtfully, and jot down any questions or comments.

This ought to make the Christian pause as he thinks about prayer. Of all the great privileges of salvation, perhaps the greatest is that God's children have an audience with the King of the universe. At any moment they can ask their Father for their heart's desire. Few of us think of prayer in this way. To most Christians prayer is a rusty tool retrieved when all else fails. Perhaps this is true because we over-complicate or have become confused about prayer.

## SOME COMMON MISCONCEPTIONS
When you think of prayer, what comes to your mind? There is certainly no shortage of confused thinking among most people. There are several distorted approaches to prayer:

▶ *The Spare Tire Approach*, for emergency use.

▶ *The Stained Glass Approach*, which requires certain "right" formulas and especially "Thee" and "Thou" of Elizabethan English.

- *The Blue Book Approach,* which views God as a college professor who grades on the number of pages you fill. The more words, the more apt God is to respond.

- *The Monte Hall Approach*: "God, let's make a deal. If You answer my prayer, I'll. . . ."

- *The Aladdin's Lamp Approach,* which sees God as a celestial genie. Rub Him the right way, and He'll grant your wish.

- *The Wrestling Match Approach,* which forcefully reminds a reluctant God of His promises and obligations.

These misconceptions are humorous until we realize they describe the way we tend to approach our Creator. Take a few moments to explore the simplicity of prayer.

---

When asked the correct procedure when someone who receives an invitation to the White House has a previous engagement, Emily Post answered, "An invitation to the White House is a command, and automatically cancels any other engagement."

If this is true of the White House, how much more the court of Heaven?

---

## A SIMPLE DEFINITION

Imagine your teenager walking up to you with this request, "O great and wise father, knower of all things, provider of my shelter and daily food, author of family order and peace, generous and benevolent ruler of the house, would you please lend me the car?" Not only would you think he was crazy, you would suspect he was up to something questionable.

When we speak to our heavenly Father in prayer, it should be as a child speaks to his earthly father. Prayer is simply *conversation between a child and his Father—verbal or non-verbal, formal or informal, public or private—concerning the topic of the child's choice.* Every newborn Christian can turn his thoughts toward Heaven to speak with his heavenly Father in prayer. It takes no special language, no specific formula, no certain place or posture. No topic is off limits. The child of God can pray *anywhere, any place, any time*, about *anything*.

## THE CONTENT OF PRAYER

There are many formulas for prayer as well as many good examples in the Psalms and other places in the Bible. Most of the great prayers in the Bible, including the Lord's Prayer, which Christ gave us as a model, contain three parts.

*Prayer should include compliments to God.* That may sound a little funny to someone raised in the church, but that is the essence of worship. Worship is paying a compliment to God. There should be a time in prayer where our concentration is on the great attributes of God's character. You could say,

> "Lord, I am so overwhelmed with Your love today."

> "Father, You are so faithful. You have never let me down."

> "Lord, I am so confused right now. Thank You that You see things clearly, Lord. You know all things."

Beginning your prayer in this way is not only appropriate to God's person, it reminds you of the greatness of the One who hears your prayer.

*Prayer should include confession.* Honesty in prayer is essential for effectiveness. I don't need to parade all my sins before others, but I do need to be totally transparent in private with God. There is, however, a time to be transparent about sin with others (see James 5:16).

Confession is not just agreeing with God that specific actions are sins, it is also admitting my need for Him.

"Father, I need Your wisdom in solving this personnel problem."

"Father, use me in the office today to draw other people to You. Only Christ can do this through me!"

"Lord Jesus, I really lost my temper with my son last night. I need Your help!"

*Prayer should include personal concerns.* When I pray, God always wants to hear what is on my heart, about *my* needs as well as the needs of others. He is eager to hear our requests. Nothing is too large or too small to take to Him in prayer.

God concerns Himself with your concerns. On any given day, we have a basketful of problems—personal, professional, relational. How foolish we are when we fail to turn to Him to enlist His help.

Don't hesitate to pray for yourself and your smallest struggle. Don't be reluctant to pray for your business: cash flow, receivables, personnel, management, development, etc. If it concerns you, God is concerned.

The Apostle Paul challenged us in Philippians 4:6-7 to take every worry to God with no thought as to the appropriateness of the request. The one requirement given in this passage is that it be a concern to *me*, His child, and that I come with a heart full of gratitude for the tremendous privilege of asking.

God wants to hear about every area of our lives no matter how complicated or trivial our concern may seem to us. As men who tend to be self-sufficient, we need to hear this. When the worries of business and life crowd in on us, many of us tend to tell ourselves, "Don't think. Don't feel. Bow your neck and stay at it!" How much wisdom, how vast the resources, how much peace of mind we miss when we bypass the opportunity to pray and try to go it on our own. God never intended for us to be able to live all by ourselves. We need Him. He is available to us even in the daily, nitty-gritty grind of the business world.

> A lady once asked G. Campbell Morgan, "Do you think we ought to pray about even the little things in life?" Dr. Morgan, in his typical British manner, replied, "Madam, can you think of anything in your life that is big to God?"

## A MATTER OF GRACE

Another crucial point: Prayer is not a reward we deserve but a *privilege* given by God. It is His gift to us, not our gift to Him. No one is good enough to earn the ear of God. Prayer is a gift of His grace. The only requirement is the Father-child relationship given to all who have received Christ by faith (John 1:12).

There is no doubt about God's unwavering love for His children. He wants to hear from us not because we are deserving, but because it simply pleases Him to do so. To attempt to earn God's ear or refuse to come because of sin is to miss the entire point of grace. Both of these responses stem from pride. Our Father calls us to believe and consent to be loved, heard, and answered even though totally unworthy of that great position.

## TIME FOR THOUGHT

Even though they worked in the same office, David's father was so busy that David had to make an appointment to get in to see his own father. Unlike earthly fathers, God is never too busy or self-important to see His children. Even while running the universe He is never distracted when we call for Him.

Day Two: Answer the following questions, and be prepared to discuss your responses. Use the suggested answers only to help you get started.

**GROUP LEADER:**
Open the group
with a short time
of prayer. Ask
those men who
feel comfortable
to share one item
they have added
to their "Personal
Worry List"
(page 95). Each
participant
should begin
keeping track of
group requests
with the "Group
Prayer Log,"
using the form on
page 93.
Read the
Scripture pas-
sages aloud in
the group and
discuss the
questions.

1. How does the privilege of prayer make you
   feel toward God?
   ☐ Grateful
   ☐ Repentant
   ☐ He cares.
   ☐ He really listens.
   ☐ He really loves me.
   ☐ I can be totally honest.
   ☐ Other (name it): _____

   _____

2. How does this make you feel about yourself?
   ☐ Secure
   ☐ Important
   ☐ Privileged
   ☐ Undeserving
   ☐ Other: _____

   _____

3. Do you ever take this awesome privilege for
   granted? Explain. _____

   _____

   _____

   _____

4. If you have ever felt unworthy of asking
   something of God, why did you feel that way?
   ☐ I had sinned.
   ☐ I wasn't good enough.
   ☐ I wasn't important enough.
   ☐ I didn't know how to talk to God.
   ☐ I felt my request was presumptuous.
   ☐ Other: _____

   _____

Day Three

5. Read back through the misconceptions about
   prayer on pages 31-32.

   ▶ The Spare Tire Approach

   ▶ The Stained Glass Approach

   ▶ The Blue Book Approach

   ▶ The Monte Hall Approach

▶ The Aladdin's Lamp Approach

▶ The Wrestling Match Approach

a. Have you ever held misconceived ideas about prayer? How did this effect your praying? _____

_____

_____

b. What is the common denominator behind each of these misconceptions about prayer? _____

_____

_____

6. Read Luke 18:9-14. How does God feel toward individuals who approach Him pridefully? _____

_____

7. Take another look at Philippians 4:6-7. What is your biggest worry today? _____

_____

Day Four

8. Think about a time you prayed honestly to God, telling Him exactly how you felt about your concerns. According to the verses we've read, what emotional doors does God open to us in prayer?
   ☐ Honesty
   ☐ Openness
   ☐ Total freedom
   ☐ Opportunity to be very personal
   ☐ Other: _____

_____

9. What kinds of feelings have you expressed to God in prayer?
   ☐ Fear        ☐ Doubt
   ☐ Love        ☐ Sorrow
   ☐ Anger       ☐ Frustration
   ☐ Guilt       ☐ Other: _____

_____

10. Is there anything that you feel uncomfortable praying about? Why is that?_____

_____

_____

_____

_____

11. Do you think there is anything that we should not pray about? Explain. _____

_____

_____

_____

_____

12. How specific do you think God wants us to be when we present our requests to Him?
☐ Keep it general, let Him decide.
☐ Let Him know exactly what you want.
☐ Other: _____

_____

Day Five: Read this section, and answer the following questions.

GROUP LEADER: This story is worth reading again aloud in the group. Take time to do that, then discuss the questions.

There is not a businessman I know who does not spend considerable time worrying about his business. Read the following account of how one man handled this.

I was trying to study the Bible and pray every night at home. My prayer time became the most important part of my day and I saw that it should start every morning. Above all, it should be a set time with no interruptions! Actually my office proved to be the best place for this; so while I continued to pray at night, I began to set aside thirty minutes or more at my desk every morning, before regular business hours. Although everyone was welcome, only Bill came at first. For months we two studied and prayed together. Gradually, others, *seeing the change in us*, asked if they could come.

Looking back, I can see that God was forming a team—and because of those He brought, we have more and more been able as a group to seek His help in policy matters and other major business problems. God wants to use different ones in different ways. I know there are more than a few groups made up of top executives and men who control the company, and also others of those in a certain department, or from the rank and file.

Usually we have at least six who attend every morning. These six include our department heads. Most of our sales managers take part whenever they are in town. A dozen or more of our men traveling all over the country and Canada also pray with us at this same hour, or during their own regular prayer times.

From the very beginning we have followed a simple pattern: we usually discuss our problems the day before, then we sleep on them. The next morning we start our day in prayer, offering up these problems to God. Each day leadership rotates to a different member of the team who opens by reading a chapter from the New Testament. Next this leader may pray extemporaneously and then he leads us in the Lord's Prayer.

In the period of silence we then offer up ourselves and our problems to God and *listen* for His answers. We always write down any thoughts and directions that come to us, and toward the end of our time together the leader asks each one to read whatever he has written. If a specific problem is not answered, or if we are in disagreement about it, we never act on it. We offer it up during the day in individual prayer and at the next meeting, until God's answer becomes clear. I do not order my executives to do anything.

We either act in love and unison, or not at all. Each meeting concludes with intercessory prayers for anyone who requests them.[1]

✣

13. Take one more look at Philippians 4:6-7. Do you think Paul included business worries in this exhortation? Explain. _____

_____

_____

_____

14. a. What business-related requests have you included in your prayers? What have you excluded? _____

_____

_____

_____

   b. Is there any business-related matter that should not be taken to God in prayer? Explain. _____

_____

_____

_____

15. How do your largest and smallest requests compare to the power of God? (Do the prayers you bring to Him support your answer?) _____

_____

_____

_____

Day Six

16. What will you miss most if you fail to pray for your work and business?
   ☐ Wisdom
   ☐ Patience
   ☐ Answers
   ☐ God's help
   ☐ Peace of mind
   ☐ Cooperation of others
   ☐ Other: _____

_____

17. What will it cost you to pray for your work?
    - ☐ Your job
    - ☐ Criticism
    - ☐ Your pride
    - ☐ Harassment
    - ☐ Personal time
    - ☐ Peace of mind
    - ☐ Others' respect
    - ☐ Other: _____

    _____

18. What is one thing that you can do to start praying more seriously about your concerns at work? Add this to your "Worry List."

    _____

    _____

## ASSIGNMENT FOR NEXT WEEK

Read the text for session 4 and work through all of the questions. Be prepared to discuss your thoughts together with the group.

Touch base by phone with your prayer partner.

**GROUP LEADER:**
Go over the assignment, then ask someone to close in prayer.

NOTE
1. John H. Ryder quoted by Harold Freer and Francis Hall, *Two or Three Together* (New York: Harper & Row, 1954), pages 73-74.

# PRAYING AS A GROUP

A man was building a tavern in a previously dry town despite the objection of a group of Christians in the community. They gathered for an all-night prayer meeting to ask God to intervene. That evening lightning struck the building and it burned to the ground. The owner brought a lawsuit against the church claiming that they were responsible. The Christians hired an attorney who denied that they had anything to do with it. When the case came before the judge he asserted, "No matter how this case comes out, one thing is clear. The tavern owner believes in prayer and the Christians do not." This humorous and probably fictitious story is an all too true indication of most Christians' belief in prayer. There is, however, tremendous power in prayer, especially group prayer, that we cannot afford to miss.

Praying aloud in a group can be a threatening experience for many people. However, Christ has made a promise that can inspire us to overcome our fear and seek others to join us in prayer—not only for His work, but our personal concerns as well. Christ says,

"Again, I tell you that if two of you on earth agree about anything you ask for, it will be done for you by my Father in heaven. For where two or three come together in my name, there I am with them." (Matthew 18:19-20)

## THE AMAZING POSSIBILITIES

The possibilities of group prayer are remarkable. Listen to what Christ is saying. Our Lord has promised to be present in a *unique way* when people, as few as two or three, join their hearts together in prayer. I say "unique" because we know that He is always present with us wherever we are. But He goes further, promising that we can be sure the Father will answer the request we agree on in group prayer.

Christ is not promising just to show up when we pray. Nor is He suggesting that we can gang up on God to coerce Him into action. I personally think that He is promising special guidance and power given *only* when Christians gather to pray as a group. When two people are impressed to offer the same request or to ask God to meet a need in a particular way, Christ is telling us that, very likely, He Himself has led them to pray in that way. We can be sure that God will answer such a prayer. *After all, it is* His request *to the Father as well as ours*. This is an assurance we simply cannot have by praying alone. It is an assurance we need in these difficult times.

## THE BENEFITS

There are other reasons why praying with other individuals is important for every Christian.

*To bear one another's burdens.* Paul commanded us, "Carry each other's burdens, and in this way you will fulfill the law of Christ" (Galatians 6:2). Obviously, this implies more activity than just prayer, as we are able, but remembering we cannot do more until we have prayed. As you pray, God may give you new insight in how to help further. As talented as we may be, and as much insight as we may have into what should be done, we still need to submit our abilities to His will and timing in purposeful prayer.

*To build commitment.* As people pray for one another, something remarkable takes place. God knits their hearts together. Read what Paul wrote to the Colossians about their friend Epaphras: "He is *always wrestling in prayer for you*, that you may stand firm in all the will of God, mature and fully assured. I vouch for him that he is *working hard* for you" (4:12-13, emphasis added). Praying together builds a remarkable bond that cannot be broken easily.

*To encourage one another's faith.* Saint Augustine defined sin as "believing the lie that you are self-created, self-dependent, and self-sustained." These thoughts are as native to the human condition as breathing. The fact is that we are desperately dependent not only on God, but according to His plan, we are also dependent on others. Even after we acknowledge our dependence on God, we often remain independent of others for many reasons. The Bible reminds us, however, that life is not a *solo* expedition.

> Let us consider how we may spur one another on toward love and good deeds. Let us not give up meeting together, as some are in the habit of doing, but let us encourage one another—and all the more as you see the Day approaching. (Hebrews 10:24-25)

We need each other for real encouragement along the way. I have found that there is nothing like praying with other men to give each of us real encouragement. We spiritually stimulate each other's faith. We are emotionally fed by the knowledge that others care about the things we are facing. Praying together also reminds us that God cares, and He can do something about our circumstances.

Whenever I acknowledge a problem to others, I am often surprised to find that several of them have been wrestling with something similar. It encourages all of us to know that we are not uniquely alone in our struggle. Paul's words remind us,

> No temptation has seized you except what is common to man. And God is faithful; he will not let you be tempted beyond what you can bear. But when you are tempted, he will also provide a way out so that you can stand up under it. (1 Corinthians 10:13)

I believe that one of the ways of escape God has designed is a group of praying men who understand the problem.

## GUIDELINES FOR GROUP PRAYER

Praying with others can be one of the most stirring experiences of life or it can be a sterile, lifeless exercise. The following guidelines are not rules but suggestions to help make group prayer the exhilarating experience God would have it be.

*Make prayer a dialogue with God.* He is present. Begin with a time of silence. Seek to feel His presence and remember what He is like. Be aware of His person and feelings as you would of anyone else present.

*Speak to God in simple words and in a conversational tone.* You are with your Father and brothers, not in a pulpit. Avoid formal, stiff, or religious language that you don't use in everyday family life. Speak to God as you would a warm, loving Father, not some austere, distant deity.

*Address God by name* as you speak: Father, Lord Jesus, Holy Spirit.

*Remember this is not a monologue.* Let others speak. Use only two or three sentences at a time, as a rule.

*Pray about one subject at a time.* Allow time for others to pray about the same subject before beginning a new request.

*Listen!* Don't plan ahead what you will say. Join in the prayer as you would a conversation. Your response can be as simple as "Yes, Lord, I agree."

*Allow God's Spirit to stir concerns as you pray*, rather than taking up time listing requests before you begin. Let the conversation take its own direction, as you would if you were chatting while on a walk with a friend.

*Pray honestly for yourself.*

*Use "I" and "me" when referring to yourself* rather than collective nouns, "we" and "us." Don't editorialize. Make it personal.

*Pray for things that really concern your heart.* A good rule of thumb is to limit group prayer to the issues you are willing to pray about personally. If your concern is not strong enough to spend your own time praying, you should not occupy the time of the group.

*Make sure that your prayers for others don't turn into a gossip session.* Take care in what you repeat about someone else. Prayer does not give you license to repeat confidential information.

*Make your requests as specific as possible.* What specific sin are you struggling with? What specific way do you want God to bless your friend? What particular action do you want God to take?

*Make your*

At the time when men first translated the Bible into English, the formal "you" and "your" were used for royalty and special formal ceremony. The familiar "thee" and "thou" were used with intimate family and friends. The translators of the *King James Bible* used the familiar, intimate language of family "Thee" and "Thou" when referring to God. They did not intend to create some formal language reserved for God, but rather used the terms a son would use for his own father in the privacy of home. When we use Thee and Thou today, we reverse the intent of the men who originally employed these terms.

*requests as big as your faith.* Limit your requests to what you believe in your heart that God could do. Don't limit your requests to what others may think.

Using these guidelines will aid you in changing your group prayer time from a humdrum, perfunctory activity that you engage in as a mere parenthesis to your meeting, to the highlight of your time together. Be patient; these changes won't happen overnight. Old patterns take time to break. Commit yourselves as a group to follow them and then give it a try.

## TIME FOR THOUGHT

God concerns Himself with your concerns. How foolish we are when we fail to enlist His help and the concerted prayer of our brothers in Christ who are ready to stand with us.

1. Have you ever been involved in group prayer? What did you like about the experience? What did you dislike? _____

   _____

   _____

   _____

   _____

   _____

Day Two: Respond to the following questions, and be prepared to discuss your answers. Use the suggested responses to get started.

2. Have you ever seen a dramatic answer to group prayer? What was that like? _____

   _____

   _____

   _____

   _____

   _____

GROUP LEADER: Move through the discussion more quickly than usual, making sure you leave at least twenty minutes at the end of your meeting to experiment with a time of conversational prayer.

3. a. What do you think are some of the reasons it is so difficult for men to pray aloud together?_____

   _____

   _____

   _____

b. How can these be overcome? _____

_____

_____

_____

_____

Day Three: Read this section, and answer the questions that follow.

Men are often reluctant to pray for *themselves* publicly or privately. I see three reasons that usually hold us back: *pride, guilt,* and *false humility.* If I fail to pray for myself because of pride, I am saying that I can take care of myself. Not only is this sinful and arrogant, it is the most *stupid* attitude a man can have. We are *absolutely* dependent on our Creator for our every breath. To say I don't deserve to make requests for myself is true enough, but to be overwhelmed with guilt is also to refuse the gift of grace that God gives through Jesus Christ. To lean on false humility, saying that I and my requests are too insignificant, is to deny the presence of the Holy Spirit within me. The fact is that you are very significant, otherwise the Sovereign of the universe would not invite you to unburden your soul. What He defines as important is important!

4. What keeps you from sharing more personal problems and requests with others? Do any of the three reasons I've mentioned hit home?

_____

_____

_____

_____

5. Are there things we should not share with others? Explain. _____

_____

_____

6. What types of requests are you somewhat reluctant to share with others? _____

_____

_____

_____

7. What could you be missing if you fail to enlist the prayer of others?_____

_____

_____

_____

_____

8. How important is group prayer to your life? How important should it be to this group in your opinion? Reread Matthew 18:19-20.

Day Four

_____

_____

_____

_____

9. How would you like the group to respond to this study? _____

_____

_____

_____

10. In your opinion, how would the group change if the content of this study on prayer became a reality to each group member?

_____

_____

_____

_____

11. Group prayer seems most effective when the group members have mutual concerns. Where could prayer groups logically be formed in your realms of influence? _____

_____

_____

_____

_____

**GROUP LEADER:**
Wait to discuss question 12 until the end of your time together, just before you pray.

12. What is one personal issue with which you can take a small risk and ask for prayer in your group? _____

_____

Day Five 13. Read through the "Guidelines for Group Prayer" again (pages 45-46).
   a. What patterns of prayer would you have to change before you are able to follow these guidelines in your small group?_____

   _____

   _____

   _____

   _____

   b. Why do you think the first three guidelines are important? _____

   _____

   _____

   _____

   c. Why are the second three important?

   _____

   _____

   _____

14. Why do you think it is important to pray as specifically as possible?
   ☐ So God will know exactly what I want.
   ☐ So I will decide exactly what I want.
   ☐ So I will be able to tell if I receive an answer.
   ☐ Other: _____

   _____

15. Why do most people tend to make requests more general?
   ☐ We are not sure of God's will.
   ☐ We don't know what we really want.
   ☐ We don't want to put God on the spot.
   ☐ We are not sure He can do exactly what we would like to ask.
   ☐ Other: _____

   _____

16. Compare the following two prayers.

"Lord, we really need to spend more time in fellowship with You. Please forgive us."

"Lord, forgive me. My perspective is out of line because I failed to acknowledge Your presence in my life this week. I have been so busy. I totally forgot You. Help me discover You today in everyday events."

a. What difference will it make to use "I" and "me" rather than "we" and "us" in prayer?

_____
_____
_____
_____

b. Honestly, would you rather be with a group of men whose prayers were like the first prayer or the second? Explain.

_____
_____
_____
_____

c. Do you have a difficult time saying "I" and "me" in prayer with others? Why is that?

_____
_____
_____
_____

**ASSIGNMENT FOR NEXT WEEK**
Read the text for session 5 and work through the discussion questions that follow. Be prepared to discuss your thoughts together with the group.

Touch base by phone with your prayer partner.

**GROUP LEADER:**
Ask how the "Prayer Experiment" is going, then go over the assignment.

Before you begin your time of conversational prayer, review three things: (1) Keep each of your prayers short and limited to one subject. (2) Give others the chance to pray about the same request before changing subjects. (3) Pray as you are prompted to say something, rather than in turn around a circle.

Ask participants to take a moment to update their "Group Prayer Log."

# MAKING TIME TO PRAY

Day One: Read thoughtfully, and jot down any questions or comments.

I am always amazed at myself. Seeing men's lives changed is a major goal for me. But even knowing that God is the only Source of true change, prayer is usually the last thing I *naturally* tend to do. I can study about prayer and talk about it, but actually praying is something else. I am a doer; I find it very natural to jump into something up to my eyeballs. I tend to plan first and then *baptize my strategies with a little prayer* to soothe my conscience. I often exhaust my own strength before turning to the spiritual resources at my disposal as a child of God. It makes me wonder at times what might have been had I stopped to talk things over with God first.

Perhaps through the exhaustion of youthful zeal, or maybe maturity, I have come to realize that my sense of accomplishment is very short-lived if I have not depended on God while doing the work, whatever it might be. Prayer is *my declaration of dependence on God.* It is my admission that all of my earthly abilities, as extensive or limited as they are, unless yielded to my Creator, will make no dent on the kingdom of darkness, which holds this world in its death grip. Prayer does not replace activity, planning, or effort, but it must precede and accompany these other pieces of the pie. Otherwise, I misplace my confidence in myself rather than in God.

## WHY DON'T WE PRAY?

Like any worthwhile activity, it is easier to talk about prayer than to pray. Very few people, it seems, have time to pray. Prayer never just happens. It is something we take time for. The real problem is not in our circumstances or schedules but in our attitude. Several hurdles chronically keep me from prayer. Recognizing and admitting these attitudes is half the jump over them.

*Prayer is work.* Paul invited the Roman Christians "to join me in my struggle by praying to God" (Romans 15:30). Prayer is the work of men not babes, of the diligent not the lazy. People who criticize those who pray as lazy have never spent much time in prayer. To spend any length of time in prayer is one of the hardest things I do. It takes all of my power of concentration to keep my attention on the business of prayer for five minutes. Why is it so hard? For one thing, prayer, while being a tremendous privilege, is our most powerful weapon against evil. Satan would rather that I engage in any activity than prayer and will always make sure there is a truckload of stresses and enticements to divert my attention.

> Martin Luther, when asked what his plans for the following day were, answered, "Work, work, from early until late. In fact I have so much to do that I shall spend the first three hours in prayer."

*I have other resources.* It is the nature of sinful man to attempt to be self-sufficient. The sad truth is that most of us will not trust God until we have no other choice. Have you noticed how much easier it is to pray when your back is against the wall? If I think, *I can do this by myself,* I will not be serious about prayer. Only when I see myself as dependent on God will I pray. The reality of the situation is that we are dependent for the very breath in our lungs each moment, much more so for the accomplishment of anything of real significance and meaning. As much as it hurts my manly pride, I cannot do anything of eternal value apart from Christ. We need a good dose of the reality of our weakness regularly, so that we can experience His strength.

*I am committed to my own comfort.* Tacitus observed, "The desire for safety stands against every great and noble enterprise." When I seek to stay within the comfort zone, avoid risk, or play it safe, I have little need to pray. Unless God graciously intrudes into my self-centered cocoon, lowers my defenses, and rolls up the safety net, what little prayer I utter will be consumed with self-indulgence. However, let me step out on the ragged edge of obedience where there are no handrails other than Christ, and praying will be as natural as breathing. If I stay far within my limits and attempt nothing that I know would take an omnipotent God to accomplish, I will not be moved to pray.

*I have isolated myself from others' pain.* Saddest of all, we do not pray because we concern ourselves with none of the world's great needs. Take off your blinders, encounter human misery firsthand, dream about what God could

---

*My creed leads me to think that prayer is efficacious, and surely a day's asking God to overrule all events for good is not lost. Still there is a great feeling that when a man is praying he is doing nothing, and this feeling makes us give undue importance to work, sometimes even to the hurrying over or even to the neglect of prayer.*

*Do not we rest in our day too much in the arm of the flesh? Cannot the same wonders be done now as of old? Do not the eyes of the Lord run to and fro throughout the whole earth still to show Himself strong on behalf of those who put their trust in Him? Oh that God would give me more practical faith in Him! Where is now the Lord God of Elijah? He is waiting for Elijah to call on Him.*

—James Gilmore of Mongolia

do through you, realize that He is your *only hope* of doing anything about the situation, and you *will* pray.

*I just don't have time.* It is rare to find a person who has more time than he knows what to do with. As Lorne Sanny suggested in his classic booklet *Making Time for Prayer*, you will never *find* time for prayer. You must make time. If prayer comes to occupy a significant place in our lives, it will be because we have dealt with these attitudes and know how desperately dependent we are on God. Prayer rarely competes with our other responsibilities. It is the one thing we can do simultaneously with all our activity. When Paul challenges us to "pray without ceasing," he is not asking us to put aside the other activities that demand our time. He is pressing us to recognize that God is there with us ready to roll up His sleeves, so to speak, and work with and through us.

## MAKING ROOM FOR GOD

Although we should set aside regular times when we allow nothing else to compete for our attention, prayer is something we make room for in our minds rather than in our schedule. The challenge is to make room in our thoughts, moment by moment, for the reality of God's presence, of our desperate need for Him, and of His willingness to work in, through, and for us.

## TIME FOR THOUGHT

Recently Fred honestly shared his concern over his lack of prayer. He said, "I have a quiet time every morning. But when I get to work, I'm so wrapped up in business that I totally forget about the Lord. I know I'm supposed to pray without ceasing, but I rarely think about God during the day much less stop to pray."

1. In what ways do you identify with Fred's difficulty? _____
_____
_____

Day Two: Answer the questions, and be prepared to discuss your responses. Remember that the suggested answers are there just to help you get started.

**GROUP LEADER:**
Begin the group
with a time of
conversational
prayer. Review
the guidelines,
especially those
of which people
need reminding,
before you begin.
*Allow as much
time for prayer
as everyone
wants.* Each per-
son should
update his
"Group Prayer
Log."
Work through the
discussion ques-
tions. To con-
serve time, you
may not want to
read the 2 Chron-
icles passages
aloud in the
group, since the
men will have
read these ahead
of time on
their own.

2. What are the biggest obstacles to prayer that you personally encounter?
   ☐ It is hard for me to concentrate.
   ☐ I tend to be too self-sufficient.
   ☐ I don't sense that I need God's help.
   ☐ I never have enough time in my schedule.
   ☐ Concerns of the day dominate my thoughts.
   ☐ Others (name them): _____
   _____
   _____
   _____

3. What does Fred reveal about his attitude toward prayer in the statement, "I know I'm supposed to pray"?_____
   _____
   _____
   _____
   _____

4. Do you agree that prayerlessness is more a matter of attitude than of circumstance or schedule? Explain. _____
   _____
   _____
   _____
   _____

Day Three

The Bible reports many accounts of men who prayed and of men who trusted their own resources. Compare the responses of two kings of Judah: Jehoshaphat and Amaziah.

5. Read 2 Chronicles 20:1-30. Why do you think Jehoshaphat sought God's help?
   ☐ He did not want to fight.
   ☐ He had no army to fight back.
   ☐ He knew God's commitment to His people.
   ☐ He thought he was up against superior forces.

☐ Other: _____

_____

6. Why was Jehoshaphat so confident?
   ☐ He knew who God was.
   ☐ He believed the prophet.
   ☐ He had confidence in his army.
   ☐ Other: _____

   _____

7. How did Jehoshaphat balance faith, prayer, action, and the abilities God has given His people?_____

   _____

   _____

   _____

8. What was the first thing that Jehoshaphat did when they returned to Jerusalem? What does this tell you?_____

   _____

   _____

   _____

   _____

9. Read 2 Chronicles 25:1-13. Why do you think that Amaziah didn't seek God's help?

   _____

   _____

   _____

   _____

Day Four

10. Where was Amaziah's confidence?_____

    _____

    _____

    _____

11. What are the biggest dangers of jumping into action before you have prayed?
    ☐ Bitterness
    ☐ Poor choices

☐ Hurting others
☐ False security
☐ Wasted resources
☐ Misplaced confidence
☐ Others: _____

_____

12. What else do you tend to depend on instead
    of God?
    ☐ Family
    ☐ Status
    ☐ Intelligence
    ☐ Personal obedience
    ☐ Financial resources
    ☐ Competence or skills
    ☐ Others: _____

    _____

13. Amaziah won the battle, but what price did
    he pay for his obedience to God's instruc-
    tions? How would this have made you feel?
    What would you have said to God?
    ☐ I am angry! Why did You do this, Lord?
    ☐ Lord, I don't understand! I obeyed You.
    ☐ This was all my fault for not seeking You
       in the first place.
    ☐ Other: _____

    _____

    _____

**Day Five**

14. Read Colossians 4:12-13.
    a. How frequently have you ever struggled
       in prayer for someone or something? ____

       _____

       _____

    b. What were your circumstances? _____

       _____

       _____

    c. What was the outcome? _____

       _____

       _____

d. What motivated you to pray this hard?

_____

_____

_____

_____

15. What are you attempting or facing or dream-
ing about that you know will take an
omnipotent God to accomplish? _____

_____

_____

_____

_____

_____

_____

16. What is the greatest human problem or need
that seems to burden your mind? What
would you do if you knew God was committed with you to tackling it? _____

_____

_____

_____

_____

17. Take a look at your own situation. Cutting
past excuses, what critical attitudes tend to
keep you from making time for prayer?

_____

_____

_____

_____

_____

Day Six: Review
the five hurdles
that keep us from
prayer listed on
pages 53-55.
Answer the fol-
lowing questions.

The Bible offers three time frames for prayer:

▶ A continuing attitude: 1 Thessalonians 5:17

▶ Daily prayer: Daniel 6:10, Mark 1:35

▶ Special extended occasions: Nehemiah 1,
Lupe 5:12-16

18. How can you make time for prayer according to the above time frames? _____

_____

_____

_____

_____

_____

19. What could you do to set up checkpoints to help you make mid-course attitude corrections when necessary to keep you in an attitude of prayer throughout the day? _____

_____

_____

_____

_____

20. At what time during the day does it make sense for you to spend several uninterrupted moments alone with God in prayer? _____

_____

_____

21. Is there some pressing issue or circumstance that calls for an extended time spent in prayer? How would you go about doing this?

_____

_____

_____

_____

**GROUP LEADER:**
Your "Thirty-Day Prayer Experiment" is more than half over. Discuss with the group members whether they would like to switch partners. Go over the next week's assignment.

**ASSIGNMENT FOR NEXT WEEK**
Read the text for session 6 and work through all of the questions. Be prepared to discuss your thoughts together with the group.

Touch base by phone with your prayer partner. If you have choosen a new partner, meet with him sometime during the week.

# THE IMPORTANCE OF PRAYER

Our culture presents us with obstacles every day that tell us we do not have time for God. Nothing could be further from the truth. We may as well say we don't have time to breathe as say we don't have time for prayer. It would not be farfetched to liken prayer to spiritual breathing. In fact, prayer is unquestionably the most vital activity we do every day. Take a moment to examine several reasons why prayer is essential to the child of God.

## WE CAN'T AFFORD TO NEGLECT IT!

*Communication is essential to relationship.* It is safe to say that for two persons to get to know each other, they must take time to communicate. In talking together they share not only ideas but something of themselves as well. Christ promised, "If you remain in me and my words remain in you, ask whatever you wish, and it will be given you" (John 15:7).

On the negative side, imagine what would happen in a relationship where two people were constantly together but failed to speak to one another or acknowledge the other's
Father is present in every place we find ourselves, and yet we act at times as if He does not exist, unconscious of His presence. This does not

Day One: Read thoughtfully, and jot down any questions or comments.

affect His unwavering attitude toward us, but it certainly affects our attitude toward Him, as well as robbing us of the joy of His fellowship, the counsel of His wisdom, and the sense of security that comes from His strength.

*Prayer is the key to Heaven's resources.* Christ taught us, "Ask and it will be given to you; seek and you will find; knock and the door will be opened to you" (Matthew 7:7). God stands ready to bless us with every blessing He can pour out upon us, but He waits for us to ask. Many of us have grown up in a culture where it was impolite to ask for exactly what we wanted. Still others feel that it is unmanly to ask for anything. To these objections James' words remind us, "You do not have, because you do not ask God" (James 4:2). Asking in faith is the key to experiencing all God has for us.

> *Always does not mean that we are to neglect the ordinary duties of life; what it means is that the soul which has come into intimate contact with God in the silence of the prayer-chamber is never out of conscious touch with the Father, that the heart is always going out to Him in loving communion, and that the moment the mind is released from the task upon which it is engaged it returns as naturally to God as the bird does to its nest. What a beautiful concept of prayer we get if we regard it in this light, if we view it as a constant fellowship, an unbroken audience with the King. Prayer then loses every vestige of dread which it may once have possessed; we regard it no longer as a duty which must be performed, but rather as a privilege which is to be enjoyed, a rare delight that is always revealing some new beauty.*
>
> —E. M. Bounds

*God loves to hear the voices of His children.* "The prayer of the upright is His delight" (Proverbs 15:8, NASB). Unlike the annoyance earthly fathers feel, far from being bothered, our heavenly Father loves to hear us call His name. We never have to call twice. He is, in a sense, already waiting for our call.

*Prayer is the key to peace of mind.* Augustine said, "You have made us for yourself, O God, and the heart of man is restless until it finds rest in you." Paul instructed us, "Don't worry about anything; instead pray about everything; tell God your needs and don't forget to thank Him for His answers. If you do this, you will experience God's peace, which is far more wonderful than the human mind can understand. His peace will keep your thoughts quiet and at rest as you trust in Christ Jesus" (Philippians 4:6-7, TLB).

*Prayer is the key to effectiveness.* Christ said, "Apart from me you can do nothing" (John 15:5). If we want God to use us, we must ask Him. If ever a man by sheer personal force, intellectual power, or natural ability could have done it alone, the Apostle Paul could have, but we see him asking for prayer in almost every letter he wrote. Our adequacy comes from Jesus Christ. We can do nothing of eternal value outside of His enablement. The fact is that we accomplish *absolutely nothing* without His enablement. Every skill we have and every resource we use comes from Him. Acknowledging this fact and requesting His cooperation adds a new dimension to even the most mundane task, to say nothing of the potential for great achievement.

> *I have resolved to pray more and pray always, to pray in all places where quietness inviteth, in the house, on the highway and on the street; and to know no street or passage in this city that may not witness that I have not forgotten God.*
>
> *I purpose to take occasion of praying upon the sight of any church which I may pass, that God may be worshipped there in spirit, and that souls may be saved there; to pray for my sick patients and for the patients of other physicians; at my entrance into any home to say, "May the peace of God abide here"; after hearing a sermon, to pray for a blessing on God's truth, and upon the messenger; upon the sight of a beautiful person to bless God for His creatures, to pray for the beauty of such an one's soul, that God may enrich her with inward graces, and that the outward and inward may correspond; upon the sight of a deformed person, to pray God to give them wholeness of soul, and by and by to give them the beauty of the resurrection.*
>
> —Sir Thomas Browne, M.D., 1605

*Prayer brings spiritual power and life to other activities.* Samuel Chadwick wrote, "The one concern of the devil is to keep saints from prayer. He fears nothing from prayerless studies, prayerless work, prayerless religion. He laughs at our toil, mocks at our wisdom, but trembles when we pray."

*Prayer is the one thing men cannot resist.* J. Sidlow Baxter observed, "Men may spurn our appeals, reject our message, oppose our arguments, despise our persons, but they are helpless against our prayers."

*God is looking for praying men.* E. M. Bounds' words remind us, "Men are God's method. The church is looking for better methods; God is looking for better men. What the church needs today is not more machinery or better, not new organizations or more and novel methods, but men whom the Holy Ghost can use—men of prayer, men mighty in prayer." There is nothing more significant than for the Author of meaning Himself to use us in one of His great agendas. Prayer is the key to usefulness.

There are so many wonderful benefits in prayer. It is amazing that we find it difficult to take Paul's advice to pray "without ceasing." Nothing but his own choice keeps God's child from enjoying this tremendous pleasure every moment of the day.

## TIME FOR THOUGHT

Day Two: Respond to the questions, and be prepared to discuss your answers. Use the suggested responses only to get started.

1. Read back through the eight reasons why prayer is essential to God's children.

    a. Assuming these reasons are all valid, just how high do you feel prayer should be in your priority system? _____
    _____

    b. Which of these eight reasons impacts you the most? Why is that? _____
    _____
    _____
    _____

2. How would making prayer a more important priority change your life?
   - ☐ Add more joy to my life
   - ☐ Bring more peace of mind
   - ☐ Heighten my effectiveness in my work
   - ☐ Increase the quality of my relationship with God
   - ☐ Give me a better perspective on my circumstances
   - ☐ Put me in touch with more of God's resources and power
   - ☐ Other: _____

   _____

3. Memorize Matthew 7:7. You can use a-s-k to help you remember—*ask, seek, knock.*

Day Three

In Eastern cultures marriages were commonly arranged between persons who had never met much less communicated together. Even in the United States during the last century we had a phenomena called the mail order bride. Instinctively we question such arrangements because we know that relationships require communication. The same is true of any relationship, especially our relationship with God. God's acquaintance is not made by infrequent greetings as we hurry through life.

4. Have you ever been able to develop a relationship without regular communication? Explain. _____

   _____
   _____
   _____
   _____

5. a. How important has communication with God been to you? Explain._____

   _____
   _____
   _____
   _____

GROUP LEADER:
Begin the group with a time of conversational prayer. *Allow as much time as everyone wants.* Review the guidelines as needed before you begin.
   Spend the rest of the time discussing the questions.

b. What correlation between communication and relationship with God have you observed in your own life?_____

_____

_____

_____

6. Read John 15:1-8.
   a. What kind of relationship does the Lord Jesus promise? What part does communication play in the development of that relationship?_____

   _____

   _____

   _____

   b. What results of that relationship does Christ desire for His disciples? _____

   _____

   _____

   _____

   _____

   _____

> *You can do more than pray after you have prayed, but you cannot do more than pray until you have prayed.*
> —A. J. Gordon

Day Four

7. Read Nehemiah 4.
   a. In facing the opposition to rebuilding the walls of Jerusalem, what was Nehemiah's course of action? _____

   _____

   _____

   _____

   _____

   b. How well did Nehemiah balance divine and human responsibility?_____

   _____

   _____

   _____

   _____

8. Do you agree with these statements? "Activity without prayer is pride. Prayer without activity is presumption." Explain.

_____
_____
_____
_____

9. Have you been guilty of pride? Presumption? Describe your situation._____

_____
_____
_____

10. What areas of your life or circumstances need this balance between activity and prayer?_____

_____
_____
_____

11. Read Philippians 4:6-7 again. Paul makes an amazing promise about peace of mind in this passage.

Day Five

   a. How would you define peace of mind?

_____
_____
_____
_____

   b. How important would you estimate peace of mind to be to most people?_____

_____
_____

   c. What does Paul suggest as the key in this passage?_____

_____

12. Has prayer ever affected your peace of mind? Explain._____

_____
_____
_____

13. a. What do you think Paul means by "peace that passes all understanding"? _____

_____

_____

_____

b. How can prayer bring this kind of peace?

_____

_____

_____

_____

14. What are some areas of your life where you need peace of mind? _____

_____

_____

_____

_____

_____

Nothing keeps the child of God from enjoying the pleasure and privilege of prayer except for his own choice not to pray.

Day Six

15. a. What will cause you to choose to take advantage of God's fabulous offer in prayer? _____

_____

b. What will stand in your way? _____

_____

_____

16. a. What five things would you like to ask of your generous heavenly Father daily?

_____

_____

_____

_____

_____

_____

_____

_____

b. What will happen if you fail to ask these
things from God? _____

_____

_____

_____

_____

## ASSIGNMENT FOR NEXT WEEK

Read the text for session 7 and work through the
questions. Be prepared to discuss your thoughts
together with the group.

Touch base by phone with your prayer
partner.

**GROUP LEADER:**
Go over the
assignment for
next week.

# PARTNERS IN THE BUSINESS OF PRAYER

Day One: Read thoughtfully, and jot down any questions or comments.

Since prayer is by nature conversation, it takes two: the man who asks; and the God who listens and answers. Our heavenly Father has enlisted us, His children, to join Him in the great business of prayer. Failure to understand either side of this partnership will not only influence the effectiveness of our prayer, it will also change the destiny of the world. The cause of Christ moves at a slow and halting pace when God's people do not pray. It is extremely important that we understand not only God's willingness to answer but also our responsibility in asking.

## THE GOD WHO ANSWERS

There is no doubt that our knowledge of God tempers our prayers. How often have we limited our requests to the size of God in our mind, or failed to ask because we doubted His willingness? Perhaps you have stayed away entirely because you felt you were not worthy, forgetting that in His grace He invites us to come despite our unworthiness. Take a moment to examine what the Bible says about the God who answers and compare this to your thoughts when you think of asking God for something.

*He is a God who is able.* God has made unbelievable promises to His children. Neither the wildest stretch of our imagination nor our courage to ask limits His ability to do what He says. Paul reminded us that God "is able to do immeasurably more than all we ask or imagine, according to his power that is at work within us" (Ephesians 3:20).

*He is a God who is eager to answer.* Far from a reluctant deity that must be cajoled or persuaded to see it our way, God is ready to hear and answer prayer. The Lord promises in Isaiah 65:24, "Before they call I will answer; while they are still speaking I will hear."

> *The Object of the prayer was a lofty one; but, lofty as it is, God is able to give more than we ask, even more than we understand. Neither the narrowness of our knowledge nor the feebleness of our prayer will limit the richness of His gifts.*
> —T. K. Abbott, writing of Ephesians 3:20

*God is incredibly generous.* Our Father usually gives us much more than we ask. He challenges us, "Call on Me and I will answer you and tell you great and unsearchable things you do not know" (Jeremiah 33:3). Nancy Spiegleberg captures this so well:

Lord,
I crawled across the barrenness to you
     with my empty cup
Uncertain
     in asking any small drop of refreshment.
If only I had known you better,
I'd have come running with a bucket.[1]

*God always gives us more than we deserve.* In calling on God's grace David affirmed, "You are forgiving and good, O Lord, abounding in love to all who call to you" (Psalm 86:5). Even when we have been unfaithful, God is ready to forgive when we call on Him. The basis of answered prayer is not our worthiness but Christ's. Paul reminded us, "No matter how many promises God has made, they are 'Yes' in Christ" (2 Corinthians 1:20).

*God is absolutely good.* No matter how badly we might want something, He will not give it if there is something better. Neither do we need to be afraid of asking for the wrong thing. Christ explains,

> "Which of you, if his son asks for bread, will give him a stone? . . . If you, then, though you are evil, know how to give good gifts to your children, how much more will your Father in heaven give good gifts to those who ask him!" (Matthew 7:9,11)

This is tremendously comforting to anyone who has a firm grip on reality. The fact is that my perspective is so limited, I am bound to pray for things that are not in others' or my own best interests even when my motives are good and pure.

*God is in control of all things.* When we come to God, we come to the right Person to get things done. Paul wrote that the Father "works out everything in conformity with the purpose of his will" (Ephesians 1:11). We are not talking to a kindly old gentleman who sympathizes with us but is impotent to do anything about it. We are addressing the God who controls and keeps everything in the universe in order.

> *To answer prayer is God's universal rule. . . . God's word does not say, "Call unto me, and you will thereby be trained into the happy art of knowing how to be denied. Ask, and you will learn sweet patience by getting nothing." Far from it. But it is definite, clear and positive: "Ask, and it shall be given unto you."*
>
> —E. M. Bounds

There is no doubt about it. The very character of God is an invitation to come to Him in prayer. David invited us:

Taste and see that the LORD is good;
blessed is the man who takes refuge in
him.
Fear the LORD, you his saints,
for those who fear him lack nothing.
The lions may grow weak and hungry,
but those who seek the LORD lack no
good thing. (Psalm 34:8-10)

## TIME FOR THOUGHT

1. What comes to your mind when you think of
asking God for something?
   - ☐ I can trust Him.
   - ☐ I'm not sure He cares.
   - ☐ What will this cost me?
   - ☐ I know He can do anything I ask.
   - ☐ Other: _____
   _____
   _____

Day Two:
Answer the fol-
lowing questions,
and be prepared
to discuss your
responses. Use
the suggested
answers only to
help you get
started.

**GROUP LEADER:**
Begin the group
with conversa-
tional prayer.
*Allow as much
time as everyone
wants.* Review
the guidelines as
necessary. Spend
the rest of your
meeting working
through the dis-
cussion questions
together.

> *What comes to mind when we think about*
> *God is the most important thing about us . . .*
> *and the most portentous fact about any man*
> *is not what he at any given time may say or*
> *do, but what he in his deep heart conceives*
> *God to be like. We tend by a secret law of the*
> *soul to move toward our mental image of*
> *God.*
>
> —A. W. Tozer

2. How do you think of God when you really
need Him?
   - ☐ He is available.
   - ☐ He is hard to reach.
   - ☐ He knows exactly what to do.
   - ☐ Other: _____
   _____
   _____

3. How does this attitude affect your prayers?
   _____
   _____

4. Read Isaiah 40:10–41:10. If your God was like this, how would it affect your prayers?

_____

_____

_____

_____

Day Three

Review the six things we said about God in session 5.

▶ He is able.

▶ He is eager to answer.

▶ He is generous.

▶ He gives more than I deserve.

▶ He is good.

▶ He is in control.

5. Which of the thoughts about God do you find most inviting to you in coming to Him in prayer? Describe how this affects you.

_____

_____

_____

_____

_____

6. What is the most wonderful answer to prayer God has given you? Do you think that you deserved it?_____

_____

_____

_____

7. Have you ever doubted God's presence or goodness because He didn't answer a prayer? What does this tell you about your view of God? _____

_____

_____

_____

8. What do the following verses tell us about God? How do they make you feel?

Day Four

Numbers 23:19 _____

_____

Psalm 86:5-7 _____

_____

Daniel 2:20-23 _____

_____

1 Peter 4:19 _____

_____

> *We tread altogether too gingerly on the great and precious promises of God, and too often we ignore them wholly. The promise is the ground on which faith stands in asking of God. This is the one basis of prayer. We limit God's ability. We measure God's ability and willingness to answer prayer by the standards of men.*
>
> —E. M. Bounds

9. What do the following verses tell us about God and the promises He made to us?

Day Five

Psalm 34:15-19 _____

_____

Psalm 37:4 _____

_____

Isaiah 65:24 _____

_____

John 14:12-14 _____

_____

1 Corinthians 10:13 _____

_____

10. a. What are the five most wonderful things that could happen to you? _____

Day Six

_____

_____

_____

_____

_____

b. Why do you want them?_____

_____

_____

_____

_____

_____

c. What is keeping you from asking? _____

_____

_____

_____

_____

**GROUP LEADER:**
Go over next week's assignment before the closing prayer.

## ASSIGNMENT FOR NEXT WEEK
Read the text for session 8 and work through all of the questions. Be prepared to discuss your thoughts together with the group.

Touch base by phone with your prayer partner.

NOTE
1. Nancy Spiegleberg and Dorothy Purdy, *Fanfare, A Celebration of Belief* (Portland, OR: Multnomah, 1981).

# THE FLIP SIDE
# OF PRAYER

W e would be amiss if we somehow suspected that effective prayer depended totally on God. God's purposes do not permit Him to answer the prayers of irresponsible children concerned only with their own comfort. Our attitude about ourselves and our needs is important in prayer. James told us that "the prayer of a righteous man is powerful and effective" (James 5:16). What are the characteristics of effective prayer? What is our responsibility?

Day One: Read thoughtfully, and jot down any questions or comments.

## THE MAN WHO ASKS

The Bible is full of models for us to observe. One of the easiest to follow is the prayer in the opening chapter of Nehemiah. Verses 1-2 tell us why Nehemiah prayed—the situation was desperate in Jerusalem. Hearing the emotional news, the only plan of action Nehemiah could pursue was prayer. He was 800 miles from Jerusalem and bound in service to a foreign king. Not surprisingly, even when Nehemiah was able to go to Jerusalem, he continued to *pray as well as work*, realizing his success was dependent on God. I find ten characteristics in this man that I would like to model.

## CHARACTERISTICS OF THE ONE
## WHO GETS ANSWERS

*Nehemiah gave his full attention to his prayer.*
As you read through this prayer, observe that
Nehemiah's whole being was involved in his
prayer—his mind, his will, and his emotions.
When he was before the throne of God, he was
all there. E. M. Bounds wrote, "It is intense and
profound business which deals with God and his
plans and purposes, and it takes whole-hearted
men to do it. No half-hearted, half-brained, half-
spirited effort will do for this serious, all-impor-
tant, heavenly business." God should wonder at
the seriousness of our desire and our devotion to
Him when we cannot give Him our full attention
as we pray.

*Nehemiah knew the Person to whom he was
speaking.* In verse 5 we see that he had a deep
confidence in the character of God. The size and
boldness of his request were based on the fact
that he knew God was a "great and awesome God"
who keeps His promises and has an unconditional
commitment to His people.

*Nehemiah made a commitment to the will
of God.* The most often repeated word in Nehemiah's prayer is

*"Nothing is impossible to industry," said one
of the seven sages of Greece. Let us change
the word industry for persevering prayer, and
the motto will be more Christian and more
worthy of universal adoption. I am persuaded
that we are all more deficient in a spirit of
prayer than in any other grace. God loves
importunate prayer so much that He will not
give us much blessing without it. And the reason that He loves such prayer is that He loves
us and knows that it is necessary preparation
for our receiving the richest blessings which
He is waiting and longing to bestow.*

*I never prayed sincerely and earnestly
for anything but it came at some time—no
matter at how distant a day, somehow, in some
shape, probably the last I would have devised,
it came.*

—Adoniram Judson

*servant.* He understood who he was; and he
understood that God was his Master. Submission
and humility are essential characteristics of

effective prayer. Today, however, many of us have reversed the roles. We expect God to be our servant; and when He does not cater to our comforts, we become angry or doubt His presence and love. Perhaps the biggest reason for unanswered prayer is that we commit ourselves to our agenda for life, not His. James cautioned, "When you ask, you do not receive, because you ask with wrong motives, that you may spend what you get on your pleasures" (James 4:3).

*Nehemiah was persistent.* He continued in prayer for three to four months before God finally responded with His surprising answer. If we really want what we are asking for, if it will bring glory to God, it is always too soon to quit praying.

At the 1992 Promise Keepers Conference in Boulder, Colorado, Wellington Boone offered this formula for how long we should keep praying: P-U-S-H, Pray Until Something Happens. That's good advice for anyone who has prayed day after day, week after week, month after month, for some heartfelt request. Have you ever said as you prayed, "God, aren't You tired of hearing this?" The fact is, you and I may be tired of asking, but we have it on good authority that God never tires of hearing His child's voice when it is lifted in earnest desire for Him to act. In Luke 18, Jesus told His disciples a parable "to show them that they should always pray and not give up." Don't be guilty of imposing your impatience on God.

*Nehemiah knew he needed God's grace.* He did not sidestep the holiness of God. He openly confessed his sin and his countrymen's sin. Our Father has every right to be offended by our sin. We have every reason to confess and be honest before God, considering His mercy and grace. If we are not honest, we lose the fellowship with Him on which prayer depends. God's plan to make us into the image of Christ simply does not permit Him to make a rebellious child comfortable by answering prayer as if nothing were wrong. Confession of our sins removes this barrier to God (1 John 1:9).

*Nehemiah asked God to fulfill the promises He had made in His Word.* He based his request to restore Israel on God's character and on His promise given in Deuteronomy 28–30. God states His desires for His children repeatedly in the Bible. We can know whether or not what we are asking is according to His will. The Word of God and prayer go together.

> *Little of the Word with little prayer is death to the spiritual life. Much of the Word with little prayer gives a sickly life. Much prayer with little of the Word gives emotional life. But a full measure of both the Word and prayer each day gives a healthy and powerful life.*
> —Andrew Murray

*Nehemiah had a compassionate concern for others.* He had a deep commitment to God's people. Although their sinfulness not only caused their problem but also resulted in Nehemiah's living in a foreign land, we see no resentment, no self-righteous attitude in Nehemiah's prayer. His response is reflective of God's gracious attitude.

*Nehemiah was more committed to God's glory than to his own comfort.* Notice his focus in verse 10. They are God's people and what happens to them is reflective on God. Although there are many other motivations for prayer, our greatest desire should be that the beauty of God be revealed to our blinded world.

*Nehemiah believed in the power of prayer.* He obviously believed that what he was doing was important enough to invest serious effort. He knew he was making a major contribution toward the solution of a seemingly impossible problem when he prayed.

> *Prayer is not the foe of work, it does not paralyze activity. It works mightily. . . . It springs activity, stimulates desire and effort. Prayer is not an opiate but a tonic, it does not lull to sleep but arouses anew for action. The lazy man does not, will not, cannot pray, for prayer demands energy.*
> —E. M. Bounds

*Nehemiah believed in a God who loves to do the impossible.* Men who pray effectively seem to have an unabashed confidence that God can do great things. Nehemiah was no exception.

Obviously, none of us fully measures up to these characteristics we see in Nehemiah. We can hope that we are moving in this direction and experiencing more and more of God's power in prayer. Let the attributes of Nehemiah's prayer serve as goals to press toward rather than standards of acceptance.

## TIME FOR THOUGHT

1. What do our motives have to do with prayer? Read James 4:1-3.

    a. What reasons does James give for prayers going unanswered?_____
    _____
    _____
    _____

    b. What seems to be James' main concern in this passage? Are there things for which you should ask that you do not? Explain.
    _____
    _____
    _____
    _____

    c. Are there things for which you should not ask? If so, what are they?_____
    _____
    _____
    _____

2. What should be your motive in asking things of your heavenly Father? How important is this to having your prayer answered?_____
    _____
    _____
    _____
    _____

3. "If we feel that we shouldn't ask for a particular thing, we probably shouldn't be involved

Day Two: Respond to the questions, and be prepared to discuss your answers. Use the suggested responses only to get your thinking started.

GROUP LEADER: Begin the group with conversational prayer. Then take time to discuss answers to prayer the group has experienced during the last seven weeks.

Spend the rest of the time working through the discussion questions.

in it or have it." Do you agree with this statement? Why, or why not?_____

_____

_____

_____

_____

_____

4. What percentage of your prayers do requests
   for yourself consume?
   ☐ 0
   ☐ 25
   ☐ 50
   ☐ 75
   ☐ 100

Day Three

5. What human responsibilities do the following
   verses reveal?
   Matthew 21:22 _____

   _____

   John 15:7 _____

   _____

   1 John 5:14-15 _____

   _____

Day Four

6. What other responsibilities do these verses
   imply?
   Proverbs 15:29
   ☐ Be ready to confess your sins.
   ☐ Realize that prayer can't be a long-dis-
     tance affair.
   ☐ Other: _____

   _____

   Ecclesiastes 5:2
   ☐ Don't be frivolous in your requests to God.
   ☐ Recognize that prayer is very important
     business.
   ☐ Put your mind in gear before engaging
     your mouth.
   ☐ Other: _____

   _____

Isaiah 55:6
☐ Don't wait until you are in big trouble.
☐ Take time to cultivate a relationship with God.
☐ Check your spare tire; it may be flat if never used.
☐ Other: _____
_____

Matthew 6:1-8
☐ Be personal.
☐ Seek answers, not applause.
☐ Find out who you're talking to.
☐ Realize that prayer is not for show.
☐ Other: _____
_____

7. How do the previous passages fit together in your mind? _____
_____
_____
_____
_____
_____

8. Read 1 Peter 3:7.                    Day Five
   a. What important factor of successful prayer does Peter alert married men to here?
   _____
   _____

   b. Why do you think this is important? _____
   _____
   _____
   _____

   c. How do you think your prayers would be hindered? _____
   _____
   _____

*There is not the least doubt that much of our praying fails for lack of persistency. It is without the fire and strength of perseverance. Persistence is of the essence of true praying. It may not be always called into exercise, but it must be there as a reserve force. Jesus taught that perseverance is the essential element of prayer. Men must be in earnest when they kneel at the footstool of God.*

*Too often we get faint-hearted and quit praying at the point we ought to begin. We let go at the very point where we should hold on strongest. Our prayers are weak because they are not impassioned by an unfailing and resistless will.*

—E. M. Bounds

Day Six

9. Read Luke 11:5-13, 18:1-8. Why do you think persistence is important to God?
□ He is hard of hearing.
□ It shows Him we mean business.
□ It teaches us something in the process.
□ Other: _____

_____

10. How long does Jesus imply we should keep praying?
□ Until He returns
□ As long as we can
□ Until we get what we want
□ Other: _____

_____

11. a. Have you ever prayed for something for any length of time? How long? For what?

_____
_____
_____
_____
_____
_____

b. Why did you persist? _____

_____

_____

_____

_____

c. What happened when you continued to
   pray? _____

_____

_____

_____

12. Do you think that more of your requests
    would be answered if you persisted longer?
    Explain. _____

_____

_____

_____

_____

13. What characteristics of effective prayer need
    work in your life? What one thing stands out
    as a real roadblock? _____

_____

_____

_____

_____

*Take time to
summarize your
thoughts.*

14. If you could choose one aspect in which you
    want to be more like Nehemiah, what would
    it be? _____

_____

15. What would you like to see the group do
    from this point?
    ☐ Take a break.
    ☐ Continue to meet.
    ☐ Start other groups.
    ☐ Meet monthly for prayer.

☐ Study a topical book together.
☐ Continue as a weekly prayer group.
☐ Study a book of the Bible together.
☐ Spread the idea of the "Thirty-Day Prayer Experiment" to other groups of men.
☐ Other: _____

_____

# APPENDIX

# THE THIRTY-DAY PRAYER EXPERIMENT

Years ago the late Sam Shoemaker challenged a group of men in Pittsburg, Pennsylvania to put God's power and interest in them to the test in prayer. These men had serious doubts about God's willingness and ability to enter into their needs and circumstances, and heal, transform or enable them in the midst of their difficulties. Each man was challenged to ask God daily, in all honesty, to meet him in his need, in spite of his doubts. The guarantee was that some kind of answer would be received within thirty days. The test worked, and spread to become known as the Pittsburgh Experiment. This section was adapted from *The Power of 30 Days* by Paul Everett (Foundation for Christian Living, 1982).

## HOW TO BEGIN A THIRTY-DAY EXPERIMENT
### One: Decide on a Specific Request
What need in your life right now concerns you most? What pressing problem(s) do you need God's help in? Write down your thoughts. Be specific.

### Two: Commit Yourself to Pray Every Day
Set aside a specific time every day, for at least five minutes, when you can concentrate fully on God and your request. Make some kind of reminder for yourself. Record it in your schedule. More importantly, pray whenever and wherever this particular need comes to mind.

### Three: Find a Prayer Partner
Identify someone who will commit to pray for you and your request every day. Exchange requests.

### Four: Take Time to Listen
Give God the opportunity to speak to your heart as you are quiet before Him. Write down any new thought or insight. Be obedient to anything you know He is asking you to do.

### Five: Leave the Results to God

Believe that God is at work even if you cannot see anything happening. Tell Him what you honestly want, but let Him choose the solution and how He will answer.

### Six: Review the Results

What has happened? Has the circumstance changed? Has your attitude changed? Do you have a new perspective?

# A PERSONAL PRAYER EXPERIMENT

## MY NEEDS

### PRAYER LOG
Mark off the days you pray.
Record any answers or insights.

1._____
2._____
3._____
4._____
5._____
6._____
7._____
8._____
9._____
10._____
11._____
12._____
13._____
14._____
15._____
16._____
17._____
18._____
19._____
20._____
21._____
22._____
23._____
24._____
25._____
26._____
27._____
28._____
29._____
30._____

**WHAT HAPPENED?**

## PARTNER'S NEEDS ℂ _____

### PRAYER LOG
Mark off the days you pray.
Record any answers or insights.

1._____
2._____
3._____
4._____
5._____
6._____
7._____
8._____
9._____
10._____
11._____
12._____
13._____
14._____
15._____
16._____
17._____
18._____
19._____
20._____
21._____
22._____
23._____
24._____
25._____
26._____
27._____
28._____
29._____
30._____

**WHAT HAPPENED?**

# A PRAYER FOR THE MARKETPLACE

**Lord, We Affirm ...**
You are the Lord of the work place as well as the worship place.
All work that meets legitimate needs is *Your* work to be done in
Your way.

Prosperity that comes from our work is a *gift* from You to be
used for Your glory, not our ease.

While You made all things for us to enjoy, true satisfaction
comes only from You.

**Lord, We Confess ...**
We have at times been proud and arrogant about success, thinking it
was because we were smarter, better, or worked harder than others.

We have sometimes placed success above integrity and power
above people. This is sin in every instance.

We have often let our love of prosperity quench our courage
and compassion.

We have kept You too often at a safe distance, mentally locked
in the church building away from our daily affairs. How we could
have used Your strength, guidance, and love at times if we had only
known You are as real a part of our lives on Monday as You are on
Sunday.

**Lord, We Ask That ...**
We, as Christian businessmen, would live ethically distinctive
lives, both publicly and privately.

We would assume the discipline of craftsmanship, working
with all our heart as if You were our boss—because You are.

We would discover what we are each gifted to do, finding the
delight and joy of doing what You created us for.

Others would see the reality of Your presence in our lives and
be attracted to You.

# GROUP PRAYER LOG

| NAME / DATE | REQUEST | ANSWER / DATE |
|---|---|---|
| | | |
| | | |
| | | |
| | | |
| | | |
| | | |
| | | |
| | | |
| | | |
| | | |
| | | |
| | | |
| | | |
| | | |
| | | |
| | | |
| | | |
| | | |
| | | |
| | | |
| | | |

# PRAYER CHAIN

Fill in the list below, making sure everyone has the same order. Use the prayer chain for requests of deep personal concern to you that cannot wait for the next group meeting. Call the person directly below your name to begin the request. He in turn will call the next person below him (last person on the list calls the first person), and so on until the request comes back to the original caller. If you cannot reach the person listed below your name, go to the next name. Leave call back messages only. Do not give the prayer request to anyone else. At a later time, try again to call anyone you had to skip.

| NAME | OFFICE PHONE | HOME PHONE |
|------|-------------|------------|
| 1. _____ | _____ | _____ |
| 2. _____ | _____ | _____ |
| 3. _____ | _____ | _____ |
| 4. _____ | _____ | _____ |
| 5. _____ | _____ | _____ |
| 6. _____ | _____ | _____ |
| 7. _____ | _____ | _____ |
| 8. _____ | _____ | _____ |
| 9. _____ | _____ | _____ |
| 10. _____ | _____ | _____ |
| 11. _____ | _____ | _____ |
| 12. _____ | _____ | _____ |
| 13. _____ | _____ | _____ |
| 14. _____ | _____ | _____ |
| 15. _____ | _____ | _____ |

# PERSONAL WORRY LIST

✔ Please place a check mark by any item too large for God to handle. In case of doubt, read Isaiah 40:10–41:10.

| DATE | WORRY | ANSWER / DATE |
|------|-------|---------------|
|  |  |  |
|  |  |  |
|  |  |  |
|  |  |  |
|  |  |  |
|  |  |  |
|  |  |  |
|  |  |  |
|  |  |  |
|  |  |  |
|  |  |  |
|  |  |  |
|  |  |  |
|  |  |  |
|  |  |  |
|  |  |  |
|  |  |  |
|  |  |  |
|  |  |  |